How to Raise a Litter of Puppies

The Beginner's Guide

CA Wilkinson

DISCLAIMER

TABLE OF CONTENTS

Author's Note

First, please spay and neuter your pets before they have the chance to produce offspring. Not only will spaying and neutering help reduce the outrageous number of animals being euthanized, but it will help your pet be healthier and happier, and better behaved.

Second, I wrote this book because there were numerous people I knew bringing puppies into this world, and most of them had no idea what they were doing. In my opinion, the puppies were paying the price for this because many of them would end up in shelters or being rehomed due to behavior problems that owners covered up, saying they just didn't have enough time for their puppy or the puppy needed more room to run.

My goal with this book is to educate people so they can raise a litter of puppies with the highest potential of staying in their original homes. Good luck with your litter of puppies, and please spay or neuter your pet after the puppies go to their new homes.

CHAPTER 1

WHELPING

1. For medium and large breeds, I highly recommend using a whelping box made from plywood. A whelping box will keep the puppies in, allow the mother to get out, and make it so much easier to raise a litter of puppies. All you need is one, 3/4" or 1" thick, 4'x8' sheet of plywood, preferably smooth on at least one side. Cut this into four equal boards, each 2'x4'. Use one of these for the entry. Cut that one in half and use hinges to connect them together so you can open and close the front of the whelping box. Then, using a 2"x4" stud cut into pieces that are 2' long, screw the plywood together so it makes a square (be sure not to affix the top part of the entry). You'll need another stud to make the pig rail which helps so the mother doesn't lie on her pups. The pig rail goes around the inside of the box about as high as the mother's backbone when lying down. Paint the inside with glossy paint so it's easy to wipe clean.

2. For small breeds, using a dog crate for a whelping box will work fine. Be sure it's a plastic one and not wire. I just take the top off the crate and it works wonderfully. The crate should be large enough to use one side as the sleeping area and one side as the bathroom area.

3. Here are some things to watch for so you'll know when your female is about to start whelping (giving birth):

- *Extreme restlessness.* She just can't seem to find a comfortable place or position.

- *Shivering.* Her temperature will drop about 24 hours before giving birth.

- *Panting.* Even though she may be shivering, she may also pant. This is a sign that whelping is not far off.

- *Not interested in food.* Usually, for about 24 hours before birthing, a mother will not want her food or anything to drink.

- *Trying to defecate (poop) and nothing happens.* This is another sign that whelping will take place within 24 hours.

4. Have her whelping box ready at least two weeks before she is due. Coax her into it and have her lie down, eat, whatever will keep her in there and help her get comfortable. You want her to be used to her box well before she actually needs to use it.

5. Don't allow her loose outside when her due date is near. She may decide to find a better place outside to have her puppies!

6. Line the bottom of the whelping box with several layers of newspapers. As she gives birth to each puppy, you can take out soiled papers and put in fresh ones. Always leave a few papers in the box that have some soil on them. Throw the soiled ones into a garbage bag and take them outside and into a trash can after the whelping is over. I start saving newspapers about the time my female is bred. Yes, this may seem like a lot of newspapers but I assure you, you will probably use them all.

7. Here is list of items I keep nearby when my female is giving birth.

- Telephone and your vet's phone number

- Pen

- Whelping chart (please see #8 below)

- Several different colors of yarn

- Scissors

- Baby scale

- A good book (for you)

- Clock

- Very soft towels

- Newspapers

8. A whelping chart should include the following information:

- Mother's and Father's names and AKC numbers (if purebred)

- Date of mating

- Date of whelping

- One line for each puppy with the following information:

- Time born

- Male/female

- Afterbirth (if the mother expelled it with each puppy)

- Collar color (each puppy should have its own color)

- Color of puppy/distinguishing marks

- Weight

- General condition of puppy

- A few lines for notes concerning the whelping

- Signs before whelping began

- Mother's reactions to her whelps

- Any issues or concerns

9. I don't recommend having anyone around when she is whelping, though having a friend with you will help ease your mind and pass the time. Whichever friend you choose, be sure it's one that your female knows and trusts. You don't want your girl getting uneasy.

10. Call your vet when she starts to go into labor. This will help your vet be prepared if you should need their assistance.

11. If it takes longer than two hours for the mother to produce another pup, assuming you know more are coming, call your vet. There may be a puppy blocking the way.

12. Most females have no problems giving birth. Just let them do what comes naturally and only step in when something is wrong. Often, a first time mother isn't quite sure of what's going on and can take too long to break the sac (if the puppy was born with the sac intact). If this happens and the puppy is moving in the sac, it's up to you to break it. Use the scissors if you have to, otherwise try to use your fingernails. It's going to be tough to break so don't give up. Break the sac near the head so you can pull the sac back so the puppy can breathe. Once the puppy is breathing allow the mother to finish. If the mother doesn't finish cleaning the pup it's up to you to do it. Simply use one of your old towels to gently, yet firmly, wipe the puppy clean. Once all the "gunk" is off the puppy use the towel to stimulate the pup. Firmly rub the puppy like his mom would lick him. Watch how she licks herself so you know how to rub the puppy. Hopefully you'll only need to do this with the first puppy. She should lick the puppy after you've placed it back in the box with her. Help the pup nurse too. Nursing will help kick in her natural mother instincts.

13. Once in a great while a puppy will be born with something wrong with it. Many mothers instinctually know this and will neglect the puppy. After the puppy is born and the sac is broken they may not continue to clean it or they may completely clean it then totally ignore it. I once had a small female

puppy born that the mother wanted nothing to do with. This was the mother's third litter so I knew something was not right with the pup. I had to break the sac, stimulate the pup, but to no avail. Every time I stopped vigorously rubbing the pup her ears, gums, etc. would turn blue. After a few hours of vigorous rubbing I realized there was nothing more I could do. This pup was obviously not ready to be in this world. She passed quietly. Yes, raising puppies can be fun, but be prepared for things like this to happen. My plan is to expect the worst and hope for the best. This way I'm not disappointed if something should go wrong.

14. Most mothers will eat the afterbirth of every puppy. I allow my girls to do this but some breeders do not. Talk to your vet about it and do what you feel best. I strongly suggest allowing her to eat a couple because this triggers the maternal instincts.

15. Don't freak out if the puppies don't look like they're supposed to. Certain breeds take time to get their spots or coloring.

CHAPTER 2

DEW CLAWS & TAIL DOCKING

Dewclaws are the nails on the inside of the leg just above the paw. Most purebred puppies have these removed around three days old. Some pups are born without them. Removing them has its advantages. If they were to get caught on something and pulled out it can be very painful for the dog. In my opinion, there is no cosmetic reason to remove them, only safety reasons. I've heard of dogs getting their dewclaws caught in fences, on trees, and in other dog's eyes. I suggest having them removed on all puppies, regardless if they are purebred or mixed breed. If you are going to have them removed make sure the vet does it when they are around three days of age. It's a very simple procedure and is done in a short amount of time.

As for tail docking, people have mixed feelings about this. It consists of cutting the tail at a certain length. You'll notice many breeds that have tails docked such as poodles and bulldogs. Tail docking is done at around three days of age, as is dewclaw removal. Many people claim this shouldn't be done because it is mainly for cosmetic reasons (making the dog look good). Others claim there are safety reasons involved in tail docking such as for hunting. Docking the tail is entirely up to you. Do some research before your litter is born to determine if you prefer the tails to be docked. Find a vet who has experience docking tails and talk to them about it. Some vets won't perform this procedure anymore so be prepared to search for a vet who will.

CHAPTER 3

WEEK ONE

1. Weigh your puppies on a daily basis and at roughly the same time every day. Record their weights on a weight chart. The weight chart is simply a piece of paper with places for you to record each puppy's weight every day for two weeks, then weekly thereafter. If any puppy hasn't gained weight you'll need to keep an eye on it. Watch to be sure it's eating and check it over to be sure nothing is wrong with it. If it hasn't gained weight or has lost weight the following day, call your vet.

2. After each puppy has been born and the mom has cleaned it, record its weight, sex, color, time of birth, and if the puppy is okay, on a whelping chart. Then, loosely tie a piece of rick-rack or yarn around its neck and record the puppy's collar color. This will help you identify each puppy at a glance, which will come in handy if you need to keep an eye on a particular puppy and later when watching litter interaction. Be sure to change the yarn or rick-rack every day.

3. Allow each pup to find its own teat to nurse. Don't give them any help. This is a natural process and each puppy should be able to eventually find where on its mother to nurse. Some puppies latch on right away and others may take a little while. If the puppy hasn't nursed after a couple hours, try to help it. If that doesn't work call your vet. Check to make sure each puppy

is nursing after birth.

4. Check to make sure each pup has a firm grasp on a nipple. Gently grab the pup and try to pull it off the nipple. You'll be able to tell if it has a firm grasp. If it doesn't, keep a close eye on it and notify your vet if the problem persists.

5. Do you want to know if your puppies are content? Listen! If they are quiet and sleeping in a loose heap, they are content. Puppies that are constantly crying are missing something. Check to see if they are getting milk from the mother. If the mother has no milk or very little milk, call your vet. They also may be too hot or too cold. If they are sleeping in a tight heap while crying, they are cold. If they are sleeping away from each other, they are too hot. Adjust the temperature accordingly.

6. Begin clipping nails about one week after birth. I use a regular human's fingernail clipper for this. Carefully clip off the curved tip, watching so you don't clip the quick (the pink part of the nail). If the quick gets cut it will bleed profusely. I suggest having some styptic powder on hand. Ask your vet for some and how to use it because it comes in different forms. Also, it helps to have someone else hold the pup while you clip the nails. My daughters do this job for me. One holds, I clip, and the other cuddles the pup that just got his nails clipped. This has also helped teach my girls how to properly handle very young puppies. Nails should be clipped at least once per week.

7. Young puppies cannot control their body temperature yet so it's up to you, the breeder, to ensure the litter is warm. If the puppies are huddled on top of each other, whining, and seem to be cold, turn up the heat a little. Many breeders place a heat lamp above the whelping box to keep the pups warm. If you do this be sure there is no way any of the pups can get their teeth on the cord or that the lamp may fall.

8. Many mothers are very protective of their new puppies. If your girl shows any aggression towards anyone, be assured that this is the reason why. I find it best to keep people away until the litter is at least a few weeks old.

9. Most mothers stay with their newborn pups nearly 24 hours per day. It's your job to encourage her to eat, drink, go to the bathroom, and maybe get a little exercise. Don't force her to leave her pups, though. As the saying goes, mother knows best! She'll eventually feel the need to eat, drink, and eliminate.

10. Even at birth, puppies have a keen sense of smell. Keep them out of garages where many odors hang in the air. You may not be able to smell them but the odors are still there.

11. Many people get worried when they see puppies "jerk" when sleeping. Don't worry! This is normal. It's just the puppy's developing nerves and muscles.

12. Young pups need plenty of sleep. Don't allow children, or anyone else, to constantly pick them up or pet them. For about 2 weeks, sleeping and eating are the two most important things a puppy needs.

13. You may find it disgusting, but, the mother will stimulate each puppy to go to the bathroom by licking them, then eating it. This is normal instinctual behavior and will continue until the pups are about three weeks old, and sometimes even older.

14. As you do your daily weighing and checking of each pup, pay attention to any pup that seems very uncomfortable at being held. This pup will need extra holding on a daily basis until it's comfortable being handled.

15. You may notice some of your puppies have a "bubble" where their belly button is. This is either a hernia or an umbilical bubble. Hernias are caused by stress to the umbilical cord, such as the mother pulling it too hard. Bubbles are caused by a fluid buildup at the base of the cord. Bring any of these to your vet's attention when you take them in for their first vaccinations. Most of these are not serious but it's better to be safe than sorry.

16. Watch your litter while nursing to be sure all of the teats are being nursed off of. If pups aren't suckling all of them, encourage them to do so. However, if the pups refuse to nurse from a certain nipple, call your vet. There may be an infection.

17. When the pups are a few days old the umbilical cord should dry up and fall off. If, before then, you notice any pus coming from the base of the umbilical try using some hydrogen peroxide on it. This should clear it up. If it doesn't, call your vet. Also call your vet if you notice any blood draining from the umbilical.

18. The first week after whelping is the most critical. Keep a close eye on the litter and the mother. If possible, take that week off work so you can observe the litter and make sure all is well.

19. Check the mother daily for the first week or so to ensure she has no abnormal discharge. Any abnormal discharge, such as pus, accompanied by a foul odor should be brought to your vet's attention immediately. Your girl may have a placenta or dead puppy still in her uterus. Also watch for loss of appetite and red, hot nipples. In short, bring anything out of the ordinary to your vet's attention. It may be nothing, but you may save your dog's life.

CHAPTER 4

WEEK TWO

1. Around 14 days of age their eyes should begin to open. Some may open a few days early and some a few days late. Never try to pry open a puppy's eyes.

2. Though their eyes are open, they really can't see anything. Give it another week or so before they begin to see a short distance from their face.

3. Their ears should begin opening around 17 days old, too; some a few days early, and some a few days late. Again, never try to pull open a puppy's ears. Serious damage can occur if the eyes or ears are pulled open. Warn children of this.

4. You can test to see if ears have opened by clapping your hands above their heads. If any heads lift you know ears have begun to open. Be gentle in your clapping. You just want to awaken them, not startle and scare them.

5. Around two weeks of age, I begin leaving the radio on for an hour or so every day. This helps the puppies get accustomed to hearing many different types of voices.

6. Towards the end of week two most puppies will have begun their first

clumsy attempts at walking. This is something every breeder should watch! Watching puppies try to walk for the first time has always been one of my favorite stages of development in puppies. Have a video camera ready!

7. After about one week most of the pups should be walking with little trouble at all. Then comes the fun part of watching them learn to run!

8. After the ears have opened, wait a few days before making any loud, sudden noises. This will give them a chance to hear what their little world sounds like. You don't want this to be traumatic for them.

9. During the beginning of the second week, begin holding puppies for about 10 minutes each while watching TV. Encourage the pup to fall asleep. This helps the pups learn to trust humans and accept handling. If any pups show agitation at this cuddling, be sure to cuddle them more often so they get used to it. This early handling will help your puppies be more friendly adults.

CHAPTER 5

WEEK THREE

1. When ears have been opened for about a week, begin making loud noises. I "accidentally" drop pots and pans, turn the radio up for a few minutes, run the vacuum, knock on doors and windows, etc. This will help them get used to loud, sudden noises so they won't fear them as adults. Don't "baby" any pup if it shows fear of a certain noise. This is just an indication that you need to make that noise more often. It also helps to make loud noises when they are doing something wonderful, such as nursing or eating.

2. Begin brushing their coats when they're a few weeks old. Doing this every day or even every few days will help them get used to the products new owners will use to groom.

3. I have found some excellent chew toys which you'll want to give them to play with sometime in the beginning of the third week. First, Chilly Bones are wonderful chewies. Just wet them down, throw them in the freezer, then give to the pups to chew. Puppies absolutely love these! Another great teething toy is the Gumabone. These come in different flavors and sizes. Rope bones are also great teething toys.

4. Around three weeks of age, puppy teeth will begin to emerge. You'll be able to feel little bumps on the gums. Within a week or so most front teeth will have come through and the tongue will have flattened out. A sign that weaning should begin soon.

5. You'll also notice that tail wagging begins around three weeks. Puppies will just stand there and wag their tails for no apparent reason at all.

6. Some puppies may have found they have a voice by this age. You'll probably hear many different yelps, yowls, barks, whines, etc. Hopefully they do this during the day!

7. By three weeks of age most puppies are able to go to the bathroom by themselves. When they do it's time to separate the whelping box into two sections. Simply lay their normal blanket on one side and layers of newspapers on the other. Hopefully they will begin to use the newspapers as their bathroom area. If not, help out by placing a few of their stools on the newspaper and by leaving a section that has been peed on. This should get the idea across.

CHAPTER 6

WEANING

Weaning involves helping puppies to stop nursing and start eating puppy food. It's not difficult and will help your female get back to her normal self. I suggest starting to wean puppies around four weeks of age. By this time their milk teeth have come in, tongues have flattened out, and they need more food than what mom can provide. Choose a day as close to four weeks as possible to start weaning. On this day, keep mom completely away from the puppies unless she is feeding them at the times designated. Don't let her see or hear them or they may stimulate milk production. Also, don't feed her at all for this day. This will help her dry up faster. The following is a suggested weaning schedule for mom followed by the suggested weaning schedule for puppies.

Mom's Weaning Schedule

- Day One – No food, limit water

- Day Two – ¾ normal food ration, limit water

- Day Three – ½ normal food ration, limit water

- Days Four, Five, and Six – ¼ normal ration

- Day Seven – ½ normal ration, continue until milk is dried up

Puppies Weaning Schedule

On the first day of weaning, I substitute one nursing for a meal of moistened puppy food. Make sure it's very runny so they can lap it up. This first meal I give in the morning so I can watch how they react to it the rest of the day. Make sure to start at least a few hours after they've nursed to make sure they're hungry. To ensure I have enough for all of the puppies I make a large batch of it. If they eat all of it I can give them more. If they don't eat it all throw away what's left in their bowl. The extra you made can be saved for the next feeding. You'll probably have to help them by sticking their muzzles in the mixture. They'll lap their muzzles and chances are they'll come back for more. This can get very messy so you may want to feed them outside or lay newspaper down under them. I feed my pups outside so they can go to the bathroom when they've finished (the start to housetraining).

On the second day, replace two meals with moistened puppy food. This works best if one meal is in the morning and the next meal before bed. Keep the consistency of the food the same; it needs to be sort of runny. Try to take them outside immediately after eating. The sooner you start housetraining the better. Allow mom to spend time with them whenever she wants to. For their proper development she needs to spend plenty of time with them. The puppies will probably want to nurse but she may refuse them. Those little teeth hurt! You'll also want to introduce them to water on this day. Just place a bowl with a little water (about 1/4 inch) in it with the pups. Make sure the bowl is shallow enough for the puppy to get out of if it falls in.

The third day you'll want to give the pups three meals. First thing in the morning take them outside to go to the bathroom. When all of them have gone, bring them in to feed them or just feed them outside (far away from where they eliminated). I find it easier to feed them outside so they can again go to the bathroom immediately after eating. The second meal will be around noon, or lunch time. Follow the same procedure as the morning meal. The third meal will be around 4-5pm, with the last meal around 9-10pm. Be sure to give them water between meals. I have used this feeding/bathroom schedule and it has worked like a charm. My pups would defecate (poop) outside all the time and not inside. Yes, they would urinate, but that's easier to clean up! All of my puppy's owners have told me how easy it was to housetrain their puppies. This is the goal because many puppies are given up, returned, sold, or whatever else because they couldn't be housetrained. The easier you make housetraining the better for the puppy. Also be sure to keep their enclosure as clean as possible.

The fourth day will be the same as the third only you'll want the puppy food mixture to be a little thicker. You want them to start having to bite at the food to eat it. It should not have any crunchy parts though. Make sure it's entirely moistened.

The fifth and sixth day consist of making the puppy food mixture a little thicker until it's like a thick paste. Don't forget to give them water to drink. They should be drinking the water with no problems by now. Leave the water for them until you feed them, and then take it away for at least an hour or so after they've eaten.

On the seventh day, continue with the four feedings but also give them a bowl with some dry food in it after you've given them the mixture (after the first feeding). Make sure the pieces are small enough for them to chew and not choke on. Leave it with them the whole day so they can taste test it.

If all of the pups ate the dry food with no problems on the seventh day, give them one meal of dry food on the eight day. On the ninth day give two meals of dry food and on the tenth day give three meals of dry food. The eleventh day will consist of four meals of dry food.

For the next few days continue this feeding schedule. At the beginning of the sixth week I get puppies used to the feeding schedule they'll have when they leave, which is a feeding around 8am, again around 1pm and the last meal around 7pm. Give them as much as they want to eat but don't allow them to act like "pigs". I like to use several different pans with food in each of them. I then set a few puppies around the pans so they don't have to compete for their food. If one pup steps into the pan I place him back on the outside. Good manners can never be learned too early. At the end of six weeks your pups should be on a normal feeding schedule of three feedings per day.

Many breeders start weaning at three weeks of age. This works well for large litters. Just follow the same guidelines above only start them at three weeks instead of four weeks of age.

CHAPTER 7

WEEK FOUR

1. If you have the available space, making a puppy play yard is an excellent way to introduce pups to many new things. Bolder puppies will help teach reserved puppies that it's okay to explore new things. Once reserved puppies see their bolder littermates explore a new item and be okay, they will be more inclined to explore that item. I suggest your play yard be at least 8'x8', though bigger is better if you have large breed puppies. Here are some things I put into my puppy's play yard:

- 2'x2' Piece of plastic (a cut up tarp works well)

- Concrete block

- Different size and texture balls (quiet and noise-making)

- Small wading pool (infant size)

- Toys hung from above

- Small sand box (around 2'x2')

- Different toys (different materials, single and multi-puppy toys, etc.)

- Block of wood

- Old tire

- Tunnels made from garbage cans or whatever you can find (no sharp edges)

- Different size boxes

I usually allow the pups to play in their yard for at least an hour every day, weather permitting. Make sure play is supervised.

2. Around four weeks old put a dog crate in the pen with them. Put some of their favorite toys in it or throw some treats in it. Have an open crate available to them at all times from here on out. New owners will greatly appreciate the early introduction to a crate.

3. I worm puppies at four weeks and again at seven weeks, just before they go to new homes.

4. Somewhere around the fourth week your pups may begin trying to get out of the whelping box. Usually, there will be one puppy that will seem impossible to keep in the box. This is when you'll either want to start putting up the hinged front of the box or move them to an area where they can't escape. I have found that the first ones to escape the confines of the box seem to be more intelligent than the other pups. It takes intelligence and ingenuity to figure out how to get out. Keep this in mind when placing your pups with new owners.

5. The fourth week is when you'll want to start introducing them to new things. Keep the introductions at home and always make it a positive experience for the pup. You don't want to traumatize them!

6. I usually start taking them outside to eliminate at this age. Weaning has begun so they will be making bigger messes. First thing in the morning I take them all out to the bathroom. It helps to have their pen by a door. As each one goes, I take that puppy back in the house to eat. This way they associate going to the bathroom outside with something wonderful, food.

Most of them go quickly after the first week because they know that food comes directly after. I take them out again around 1pm, 5pm, and again around 9pm. On this schedule most of my pups will wait until morning to go again. They will probably pee in the box though. Keep their pen as clean as possible. This helps promote good bathroom habits.

7. Once you start to wean the pups, you'll need to give Mom access to an area where she can be away from the pups yet go to them if she wants. They still need their mom!

8. Mom will probably begin to discipline them around four weeks of age. This usually involves her showing her teeth, growling, and/or snapping at the pups. Don't worry about this. This is normal canine behavior. It teaches the pups what they can and can't do, and also how to read canine body language. This is very important so never scold the mom for scolding her pups.

9. Once you start weaning them, use a specific sound right before you feed them. I use a squeak toy. I give the toy a few squeaks then put the food down for them. They learn very quickly that when they hear the squeaks food is coming. Use this for teaching them to come, too. When I have the pups outside for play sessions I give a few squeaks a couple times. When they come, and they will, I give them plenty of love and praise. This lays the foundation for teaching a reliable come when they're a little older.

CHAPTER 8

WEEK FIVE

1. Around five weeks of age, begin taking individual pups for car rides. If you go to the bank, take a pup. If you go to the post office, take a pup. It helps to have someone with you to hold the pup during its first few rides. Holding it will make it feel more secure and comfortable. Don't allow it to jump around and play. Usually, the first time one of my pups goes for a ride I just drive around the block, come back for a different pup, and so on. This way all of them are introduced to the car on the same day and it gives me an idea of which puppies need extra time to get used to it. Try to take pups for rides every few days until they go to their new homes.

2. Don't try to force an object onto them. They will get used to it in their own time. Just allow them to see the object, smell it, and walk up to it. When they do all of these things give them some praise.

3. Think of things your puppies will encounter when they go to new homes and try to introduce them to these things a few weeks before they go to new homes. Examples include: lawn mowers, vacuum cleaners, cats, cattle, birds, other types of pets, etc.

4. I usually give my pups a few baths before they go to new homes; the first one around five weeks of age. Make these baths as enjoyable as possible

with lots of praise, petting, and treats. I normally don't use any shampoo, just running water over them accomplishes the same thing. Be very gentle and encouraging.

5. Around five weeks of age I put the adjustable quick-clip collars on the pups. Most won't have too much of a fuss because they've been wearing the yarn collars. Just give each puppy as much time as it needs to get used to its new collar. It will help to let each pup sniff it before you put it on.

6. As for vaccinations, I give a parvovirus shot at five weeks and the puppy shot (DHLP) at seven weeks. Don't worm and vaccinate a puppy on the same day. If they have a reaction you'll know exactly what caused it.

7. While the pups are eating, make different loud noises. This will help the pups associate loud noises with something great-eating! Thus, the pups won't be fearful of sudden loud noises. This is especially helpful when raising puppies that will be hunting when they get older.

8. It's usually around this time that your children will want to really start playing with the pups. This is okay, but warn them not to lie down. Puppies love human hair and a child could easily get injured by puppy teeth and claws on their heads.

CHAPTER 9

WEEK SIX

1. Help your pups get used to going up and down stairs. Of course, if you're raising a small breed litter this will be up to the new owners Start with just one or two steps. Do everything you can to coax the pup up (treats, mom, toy, sibling, etc.). Really praise if he makes any progress at all. Don't worry too much if they resist. Every pup will eventually learn to go up and down stairs. The point is to introduce them to it.

2. Once they've become used to the collar it's time to introduce the leash. Work with only one pup at a time. Attach the leash to the collar then just walk around. Most likely the pup will follow you, getting used to the leash at the same time. Once the pup will readily follow you, pick up the leash and walk. Having them walk nicely at heel is not the goal, but rather to give them the opportunity to get used to the leash. Don't expect too much from young puppies. Please read #5 in Week Seven for another way to leash train young puppies.

3. Now that the pups are getting their personalities, you should be able to tell which ones are submissive or shy. Help these puppies come out of their shell by spending a little extra time with them daily by playing and cuddling with them. Do what you can to get her to be playful and outgoing.

4. The sixth and seventh weeks are the best time for you to teach your puppies manners and obedience, and to socialize them with humans. Puppies' brains are like sponges just waiting to be filled up. The more you teach them in these last two weeks the better adult dogs they will be.

CHAPTER 10

WEEK SEVEN

1. I worm puppies at four and seven weeks, just before they leave for new homes.

2. As for vaccinations, I give a parvovirus shot at five weeks and the puppy shot (DHLP) at seven weeks. Don't worm and vaccinate a puppy on the same day. If they have a reaction you'll know exactly what caused it.

3. Don't allow your pups to leave home before they are seven weeks old. They need a full seven weeks with their mother to help them learn how to be canine. If they leave before seven weeks they may end up being aggressive towards other dogs or have other behavior problems.

4. Assuming you've allowed them access to a crate the past few weeks, you should now be ready to start crate training. Take two puppies away from the others, outside if the pups are inside. Place both pups in the crate with some favorite toys or some food. Close the gate for a few seconds. If they don't react, close it again. Keep it closed until you feel they will either scratch at the door or start crying. Before they get the chance to do either, open the door and let them out. Give them some treats and lots of praise. Do this with all of the puppies just making sure that at least two are in at the same time. Continue doing this until you can close the door for a few

minutes without them throwing a fit. Keep them in the crate as long as they'll remain quiet and calm. Don't forget to give them toys that will keep them busy for some time such as the Chilly Bone, Kong toy filled with peanut butter, or a natural beef bone filled with peanut butter. You want them to associate the crate with something good so always make their crate time a positive experience.

5. One of the easiest ways to leash train a puppy is to attach two littermates of equal size together by a cord attached to their collars at least 1-2 feet long. They will probably start by pulling against each other. But before long they will realize to go with the force of the cord. When this happens it's time to attach the leash and take them for a walk. New owners will love you for teaching your pups to walk on leash.

6. It's easy to get caught up in the moment with puppies that are seven weeks old. But don't let anyone rough house with them. Rough housing will cause the pups to use their teeth on humans; something that isn't allowed when raising any puppies.

CHAPTER 11

OTHER STUFF

1. Don't use crates as punishment. The crate should be a safe and pleasant place for the puppy.

2. Let your puppies experience as many new things as possible while they're young. Go for car rides, let them walk on new surfaces (gravel, plastic, pavement, etc.), anything that "broadens their horizons". Don't baby them if they show fear though.

3. Never feed your puppies table scraps. This isn't healthy for puppies and it also teaches them that it's okay to eat food other than puppy food.

4. Here are toys that I recommend for puppies or adult dogs: nylon bones, gum bones, food cubes or balls, hard plastic balls your dog can roll around, sterilized natural beef bones, tennis balls, Frisbees, rubber toys, and retrieving dummies.

5. When puppies sleep they sometimes move. This may look like he's shivering or shaking, making you think he's having a seizure or something. They generally kick their legs as if they were chasing something in their dreams. They may also make little noises like whines or muffled barks. This is quite normal. If this worries you though, take your puppy to the vet to

ensure he's healthy.

6. Massaging puppies is an excellent way to get them used to human handling. Start with the head, and then go to the ears, neck, shoulders, front legs, back, sides, and hips. You'll notice puppies starting to nod off and close their eyes when you start. This is a good sign that the puppy is comfortable with humans handling it.

7. When puppies bow down (front legs on the ground, hind legs perpendicular to the ground), they're saying they want to play.

8. Keep your puppies under control at all times for their safety and others'. This means keeping them in a fenced area outside.

9. Keep a current photo of each of your puppies and record distinguishing marks. These photos and records will help if a puppy is ever lost or stolen.

10. A permanent form of identification is tattooing. Many people put the tattoo on the inside of the ear but I prefer putting it on the inside of the thigh. Ask your vet if they have the necessary tools to perform tattooing or you can look in pet stores, pet supply catalogs, or ask a breeder.

11. Be sure to puppy proof your home before allowing any puppies to roam outside the whelping box. The easiest way to do this is to lie on the floor in each room and scan the area from the floor to about three feet up. Hide electric cords, put up plants and breakables, put away any rodent poisons or traps and cleaners, and anything else within a puppy's reach that you don't want eaten, destroyed, or a puppy harmed by.

12. When puppies need sleep, they sleep. You may be playing with your puppies one second and the next they're sound asleep!

CHAPTER 12

A LITTER OF ONE

1. Place a few stuffed animals in the whelping box with the pup. When it's feeding time, use these toys to sort of push the pup like a littermate would. This gives the puppy mild stress which is good for it. Even while the pup is nursing use the toys to push against it. In other words, do like a littermate would and try to steal the pup's nursing space. Be gentle yet firm. You want to give it mild stress yet let it eat at the same time.

2. As the puppy gets to be a few weeks old, you'll want to add a few more stuffed animals. Something that will make it have to climb over, or compete with, to get to mom to nurse.

3. It's very important to allow the puppy to spend as much time as possible with mom. Since there are no other puppies for it to learn from, mom will have to do this task. She will help teach it such things as dominance, submission, good behavior, and unwanted behavior. Allowing it to spend time with dad will help, too.

4. I suggest giving the pup its first parvovirus vaccine at five weeks of age. A few days after giving the vaccine, try to find other puppies for it to play with. Another litter of pups for it to interact with is ideal. But if you can't find a litter, try finding three or four people with puppies your puppy's

approximate size for it to play with. It's vital for your puppy to have interaction with other puppies. They will help teach it how to behave like a dog.

5. Don't give your pup too much human attention before week six. It's more important for it to interact with other dogs at that time. I don't mean to ignore it, but rather give it plenty of love and attention, and at the same time, give it plenty of opportunities to play with other puppies or small dogs.

6. Let the new owners know that their new pup was an only pup. Let them know how important it is for their pup to be socialized with other dogs. Failure to do so can lead to a dog who doesn't know how to "speak" dog which can cause problems in the future.

CHAPTER 13

ORPHANED PUPPIES

Raising orphaned puppies can be very difficult or very easy, depending on the age they were orphaned. Puppies that lost their mom at birth or within the first few weeks will need a human to care for them nearly 24 hours per day, seven days per week, for the first few weeks. Here are some suggestions to help you raise a litter orphaned at birth or before three weeks of age. Yes, there will be information on puppies orphaned after three weeks, too. Read on! Also, be sure to read the suggestions in the other sections of this guide. You'll find plenty of information that can help.

1. Newborn puppies basically need four things; warmth, sleep, food, and elimination (go to the bathroom). It's up to you to provide these things since their mother can't. We'll start with warmth.

- *Warmth*. Keep them somewhere warm and away from doors and drafts. A warm litter will lie in a loose pile. A cold litter will lie in a tight heap while shivering and whining. Adjust the temperature according to how your litter acts.

- *Sleep*. For the first few weeks they will need plenty of sleep. Other than feeding them, helping them to eliminate, and doing the daily weighing and checking, they'll sleep.

- *Food.* Newborn pups will want to eat every few hours. Be prepared to feed them at least every two-three hours for the first week. This includes getting up in the middle of the night. To feed them you'll need newborn animal bottles and at least two nipples per pup (in case one breaks or gets chewed). So if you have six puppies I suggest having at least three bottles and 12 nipples. When you get the bottles, purchase the formula for newborn puppies. Your vet will be able to help you with this or your local pet store. It may take a few tries for the puppies to get used to suckling from a bottle, but don't give up. When you're nursing the puppies, hold them in a position that they would normally nurse from their mom. Don't hold them on their backs-hold them under the belly and let them nurse in a horizontal position. For socialization purposes, have a friend or family member nurse another puppy next to yours so they get the mild stress normal nursing would provide. After two weeks they should be able to go at least three to four hours between feedings. Listen to them, if they're whining and crying, feed them. Continue to bottle feed them until they're at least three weeks old. By then their tongues will have started to flatten and teeth will be coming in. You can start them on gruel. Please read the section on weaning to learn how to get the puppies to eat on their own.

- *Elimination.* Normally their mom would do this. It involves stimulating the genital area to get them to go to the bathroom. Since mom isn't able to, this is your job, and yes, it must be done. Moms normally do this before, during, and after feeding time. All you need to do is moisten a couple paper towels or use baby wipes and gently rub the puppy's genital area in the same manner the mother would lick. Chances are it will urinate and defecate almost immediately. Keep rubbing until the puppy completely stops. It helps to place something under the puppy that you can throw away afterwards. Use a new paper towel for each puppy. I suggest doing this before you feed each puppy and again after it has nursed. This is an important step so don't forget to do it. Yes, it sounds disgusting, but your pups would probably die if you didn't do it. So grab those paper towels and get rubbing!

2. Watch your litter to see how they are doing. Are they loosely lying in a

heap? Are they sleeping quietly? Are they gaining weight? If you can answer these questions with "yes", then I'd say you're doing a good job! Keep up the good work. However, if they're crying, whining, or huddled together, then something is not right. Go over the suggestions above and see if you can fix the problem. If not, call your vet immediately.

3. It's very important to weigh your pups every day. Use a weight chart to record daily weights of pups up to at least two weeks of age. Weighing weekly thereafter is okay. If any aren't gaining weight or are Losing weight I suggest calling your vet.

4. If your pups lose their mom after three weeks of age you can start them on gruel instead of bottle feeding. Follow the steps in the weaning section. You'll also want to find an adult dog for them to interact with on a regular, daily basis. Find a dog that would be about the same size as their mom and is in good health. Be sure it's had all of its shots and has no parasites.

CHAPTER 14

FINDING NEW HOMES

1. Start advertising your litter as soon as they're born if you don't already have homes lined up. This will give you plenty of time to find homes and talk to prospective owners.

2. If someone wants to reserve a puppy and you agree they will give your pup a good home, have them fill out a reservation form. This is a form stating that a certain individual has chosen to purchase a puppy from you and has made a deposit of X amount and that you agree with it. This will ensure they get their choice of puppy and you know that one has a home. If the pups are under six weeks of age don't allow them to choose a specific puppy but rather their choice of first female, first male, second female, second male, etc. Puppies under six weeks of age haven't developed enough for anyone to choose. Usually, people place a small deposit for you to hold either their pick choice or a specific puppy. If you're giving your puppies away, have them give a small amount of around $20.00 to hold their choice (give it back when they pick up their puppy). Normally, this amount is nonrefundable should they change their mind. If you sell your pups, this deposit would be put towards the purchase price.

3. Here are some questions you should consider asking prospective buyers before they reserve or buy a puppy. From their answers, and questions of their own, you can decide if they should get one of your babies.

- Have you ever owned one of this breed before?

- Are you prepared for the amount of exercise/grooming it requires?

- Who will be the main caretaker?

- Where will it spend most of its time?

- Where will it sleep at night?

- Do you have the time to housetrain and obedience train it?

- Do you have a vet or have you found one yet?

- Have your children been around dogs before?

- Do you have the financial means for proper vet care?

- Why do you want this breed?

Their answers should give you an idea of how they would care for your puppy. Ask as many questions as you would like. This is a lifelong commitment here!

4. When I first meet people looking at my pups, I give them some time to ask me questions. No, I don't ask them if they have any questions. I just start talking about my dogs and the puppies. In my experience, people who ask numerous questions have done their homework and are ready to get a puppy. Those who ask little or no questions aren't prepared for having a puppy yet. Prospective owners should have already done some research on the breed (or breeds if the litter is mixed) and should know about how big it will get, the amount of exercise it needs, and so on. If people are asking you general questions like, suggest they research the breed and get back to you in a few days if they still feel one of your puppies would be a good fit for them.

5. I let my dogs help me choose new owners! Before anyone gets to see the pups they must meet the parents. If my dogs take to them right away they have a good chance of getting one my babies. If my dogs are reserved around them or continually bark at them, chances are they won't get a pup. I like to think my dogs are excellent judges of character! The last litter I had, my dogs took to everyone that came to see the pups, with the exception of one person. As soon as this person got out of the car they growled at them and continually barked. There was something about this person my dogs didn't like so I told the person that I would give them a call with my decision. Needless to say, they didn't get a puppy. Trust your dog's instincts. They can sense things about humans that we can't.

CHAPTER 15

VET VISITS

1. Unless your puppies get their dewclaws removed, tails docked, or if you follow my vaccination schedule, their first visit to the vet should be around seven weeks. At this time the vet will check them all over and give them their first vaccination and will probably worm them. If there are any problems, you will know before they go to new homes.

2. If any of your pups have a problem, it is your responsibility to inform the new owner. If they choose not to take the pup because of a problem, you should give them their choice of another pup.

3. Before you leave the vet's office you should receive a certificate for each puppy stating its health. This form should be given to the new owners as testament to the puppy's health.

4. Most vets will also give you a starter packet for each puppy. Give these to the new owners. They contain useful information such as pet health insurance.

5. If your vet worms the pups, ask him to send another dose home with you. This way if you have any puppies left you will have the wormer and won't need to visit the vet again.

6. If you have noticed anything strange about a puppy, bring it to your vet's attention. He may not notice it since it may not be part of their normal examination process. However, most vets should notice anything visible to the human eye.

CHAPTER 16

LITTER MINGLING

Litter interaction the first few weeks consists mainly of the pups using each other for warmth and fighting for nursing space. The stronger pups will get the best teats while the weaker ones fight for them. Once eyes have opened and they begin to walk, there is much more litter interaction. You'll see pups chewing on ears, tails, or anything else they can get their teeth on. Because teeth haven't fully come in yet this chewing doesn't hurt. Once teeth are in, pups learn that their chewing another pup does hurt. The pup being chewed will yelp and try to get away.

This is when you'll begin watching the litter to determine which pup is most dominant, submissive, independent, etc. Dominant behavior includes one puppy standing next to and placing his paws on another puppy's back, standing stiff-legged with tail raised, and pushing another pup. Keep notes so you'll know which pups display this behavior; it helps when people are choosing their pup. For example, a shy person would not work well with a very dominant puppy. And the same for submissive pups-a very loud person would not work well with a submissive pup. Independent pups usually do their own thing. These are the pups that wander away from the litter and explore whatever they want.

In the beginning of the third week you should give the pups toys to play with. They'll use these toys to play with, learn who is the strongest, and for learning general dog behavior. One pup could be playing with a toy when another pup takes it away. The pup will try to get it back, thus learning if he is stronger or weaker. One pup will start playing with a toy and before long every pup in the litter wants or has had the same toy.

You may encounter puppy fights every now and then. These are perfectly normal. It's simply two pups trying to determine who is more dominant. They usually only last for a few seconds. Don't break it up unless it goes on for more than a few seconds. If you need to break it up don't pick up one pup or try to use your hands to separate them. Drop something near them to get their attention. If you use your hands you may get bitten. The pup that loses may run away crying like he's nearly been killed, but generally these little fights are nothing more than the pups snarling and pushing each other. It's important to allow these dominance fights to occur so the pups learn who is dominant and who isn't. This is a natural learning experience for all puppies.

Puppies will learn from each other what different body postures mean. They'll learn that bowing down invites play or that standing tall with tail raised either makes another pup walk away or start fighting. They learn that staring at another pup makes that pup either look away in submission or stare back until they, themselves, turn away. It's all part of the language of dogs.

If you sit down and watch a litter interacting, you'll notice all the different body postures and how the other pups react. Keep notes of each pups unique personality so you can relay that information to prospective owners. They'll really appreciate the time you took to recognize each puppy's temperament.

CHAPTER 17

MOTHER & LITTER MINGLING

Throughout the entire seven weeks the puppies are with you it's vital for the mother to spend as much time as possible with her pups. Not only will she provide food, warmth, and protection in the early weeks, she will also teach her pups how to be dogs. Puppies are born with numerous instincts, but reading another dog's body language is mostly learned from their mother and littermates. You'll notice the mother will growl at, pin down, and may scruff shake when the pups are older. Don't think she's being mean or moody. She's simply teaching her pups what is, and isn't acceptable behavior. I know of one mother who even knocked her pups down if they jumped on someone!

When weaning time comes the mother may growl and walk away if the pups try to nurse. This is her way of naturally weaning the pups. Once weaning is complete and the pups are on dry puppy food, it's very important to let the mother (and father if possible) have plenty of interaction with the pups on a daily basis. Give them plenty of toys to play with, too. I usually give a couple sterilized, natural beef bones to them in addition to other toys. Chances are the mom will settle down with a bone and teach the pups that stealing will not be tolerated. She'll probably growl the first time and if that doesn't work to keep a pup away, she may give a quick snap. This won't hurt the pup though it may sound like she just tried to kill him. Allow this interaction to occur. Don't interfere and don't coddle the corrected pup. Let him handle it on his own. Generally the mother's quick snaps never produce blood. It's only meant to discipline the pup and they usually catch on right away.

When you're introducing the pups to new things having the mother around can help tremendously. She will help show the pups they have nothing to fear. Just her presence is enough to reassure a puppy to explore the new object or surrounding. However, if there is something that she fears don't have her around when you introduce the pups to that object, surrounding, or noise.

If you plan on keeping any pups or if any pups are still with you past seven weeks of age, I suggest keeping the mother and pup(s) separate for at least one week. This gives the pups an opportunity to bond with humans and develop their own personality. If you can separate them for more than one week it would be even better. When they get back together it's probable that none of them will act like mother and pups. Instead, they will react like canines that have met for the first time. They will do the usual sniffing and the pup will probably show submission by lying on its back and exposing its belly.

Trust your female dog's instincts when it comes to raising pups. The old saying "mother knows best" is true when it comes to raising a litter of pups. Though you may not agree with her methods of discipline, I assure you she does them for a reason. It's extremely important for mothers to discipline and play with their puppies. She is the main thing for teaching puppies how to behave like dogs. As long as the new owners continue socializing their pup with other dogs and puppies, they should have an adult dog that can play with and be trusted around other dogs of any shape and size.

CHAPTER 18

HUMAN & LITTER MINGLING

The first three weeks should involve you weighing and checking the pups on a daily basis. I'm sure you'll hold and pet the puppies too. I mean, who can resist holding little puppies? Around four weeks of age you'll start weaning, which will give the pups more time with people. The last few weeks the pups are with you should involve plenty of human interaction. Not only should you be introducing them to new things, but you should also be teaching them about humans. It's your job to start teaching them that biting humans hurts. When pups bite me I gently, yet firmly, grab their muzzle and give a little squeeze. You'll have to do this on an almost continual basis because puppies explore nearly everything with their mouths. Don't allow them to chew any of your clothing either. If you start teaching them early the new owner's job will be much easier. You should also start teaching them that jumping up is wrong. Gently push them down if they jump up.

You'll be teaching them manners and you'll also have to teach them that humans are wonderful. Spend plenty of time playing with them using their toys or just petting them. Hold them against your chest and cuddle them. Help them get used to being handled. Invite family and friends over to spend time playing with your pups. Try to get people of all ages, male and female. This helps them get used to different people and voices. You should also wear different clothing around them so they get used to different clothing styles and won't show fear of some new piece of clothing. These articles of clothing should include baggy pants, baseball caps, big straw hats, bulky coats, boots, or anything that makes you look different. Use your voice to calm the pups if they bark at you. Don't pick any of them up until they recognize you. Your point is to help them get used to different clothing, not terrify them!

I like to set up times every day for people to play with my pups. This is never a problem since most people I know love to play with little puppies! Be sure to supervise any play with your puppies and children. Sharp teeth hurt! Be sure to speak up if someone handles a puppy roughly and seems to be scaring a puppy. It's very important for all human interaction to be positive and wonderful for the pups. You want them to adore being with people. Keeping everything positive reinforces the idea that humans are wonderful. If a puppy should somehow be frightened by a human, let him deal with it in his own way. Once he's calm, have the same person just sit down near the puppy and offer some treats or a favorite toy. Let the pup take his time warming up to the person. Don't let the person leave until all has been "forgiven" by the puppy.

Most importantly, have fun with your puppies and spend plenty of time playing with them. The more humans they see and play with the better. In a society where dog bites are becoming more common it's vital to your pups' lives to have them interact with as many people as possible. Be sure all new owners are aware of what socializing with humans is and that they are prepared to do everything they can to continue socializing their puppy. Your puppy's life depends on it!

CHAPTER 19

TEMPERAMENTS & HOME PLACEMENT

Helping new owners pick their puppies is something every litter owner should do; regardless if the pups are purebred or mixed breed. Since you've spent the last seven weeks with the pups you know more about them than anyone. You should have been keeping notes on each puppy for the last week or so you'll know which puppy is most dominant, submissive, independent, etc. If you have already met with people who are taking your pups you should have a general idea of their situation and can make a recommendation as to which pup you feel will fit best with them. Let them know your suggestion and why you feel that particular puppy would work best for them. Most people appreciate this information. I have yet to come across a person choosing one of my pups that didn't appreciate my suggestions.

I suggest not allowing a shy, soft spoken person to take a very dominant puppy. This mixture could be devastating in the future. Instead, suggest the very friendly pup that seems neither dominant nor submissive. For a family with children I would suggest the puppy that loves to be near people and is always getting underfoot when you walk. For an elderly person I would suggest a somewhat submissive puppy. Suggest the independent puppy to the very active, always on the go type of person. This pup will get so much exercise that the wandering won't have a chance to occur!

Some breeders may choose not to help people pick their puppies and this is okay. I still suggest letting people know what you know about each puppy's temperament. And don't allow a family with children to take a very dominant puppy.

CHAPTER 20

AKC REGISTRATION

If you are raising an AKC (American Kennel club) registered litter you'll need to contact the AKC for a litter registration application. Visit their website at www.akc.org to request an application or, to make things easier, complete it online. About one week after the pups are born fill in the necessary information and mail it, along with the fee. In a few weeks you should receive individual registration forms for each puppy. Check them over to be sure the information on them is correct and fill in any information requested. Now you'll need to decide if you want any pups to be granted Full Registration, which means the owner can show them in conformation and obedience, and can breed them. The other choice is Limited Registration. With Limited Registration the puppy cannot be shown or bred without you, the breeder, removing the Limited Registration status. I highly recommend placing all puppies on Limited Registration. If a puppy is good enough to be shown or bred you can always remove the Limited Registration and grant that puppy Full Registration. Whichever registration you choose, be sure you let the prospective owners know before they reserve or buy a puppy. When each puppy is picked up be sure you've filled out the necessary information and checked either Full or Limited Registration. Once the new owner has the AKC application it's their responsibility to register their puppy.

CHAPTER 21

HEALTH & SALES CONTRACT

Most purebred puppies are sold with a health and sales contract, which means you, the breeder, are responsible for genetic health problems until a certain age. Most contracts are valid until two years of age and some are valid until the dog passes on. Your health contract should allow the new owner to take the puppy to their vet for an exam and return the puppy for a full refund within 48-72 hours. Keep in mind that health and sales contracts are meant to protect the new owner, as well as the puppy. I include a section in mine that if one of my puppies is caught being abused I will take that puppy at no cost to myself. It also states that no puppy of my breeding will ever step foot inside an animal shelter and that I have first choice to buy back the puppy should the owner decide they can no longer keep the puppy. This section shows that I care about my puppies and will be there to help, no matter what. You'll also want to include a section for spaying and neutering in your contract. Offer a rebate upon proof of spay or neuter by a certain age (usually by one year of age). Be sure to have two copies for each person to sign, one for you and one for them.

CHAPTER 22

MIXED BREED PUPPIES

Mixed breed puppies may look like their mom one day, dad the next, and something entirely different the following day! You just never know what a mixed breed puppy will look like when full grown. Just because he has short hair now doesn't mean he'll have short hair when an adult. Explain this to people who are interested in your puppies. If they want a certain look in a dog maybe they should look for a purebred with the looks they like. Personally, I feel half of the charm of mixed breeds is the surprise of what it will look like full grown!

You'll also want to let new owners know that, in general, mixed breeds enjoy healthier lives than purebreds. This is due to something called hybrid vigor. New owners will be glad to hear they can expect a lower vet bill than if they had bought a purebred!

In light of today's pet overpopulation problem, I suggest you ask new owners to spay or neuter their puppies. Offer them a rebate of say $25.00 upon proof of spay or neuter. If you can't afford to give money away, ask new owners for a spay/neuter deposit of $25.00, refundable when you receive proof of the puppy's spaying or neutering. Any owner who cares about their new puppy will not have a problem with this.

CHAPTER 23

THE FINAL DAY

This can be a very emotional day, depending on your personality. It helps to have found wonderful people to take your pups. Instead of feeling like you are losing your pups you'll feel like you're gaining friends. Before the pups leave for their new homes be sure all of them are clean. If necessary, give baths to any who may need one. Depending on the time they'll be picked up, try not to feed them just before they leave for new homes. I find that feeding them first thing in morning will hold them over until they get to new homes. Once they're in their new home have the buyer feed the pup to help him relax. Before you let any of them leave, here are some things that you should have ready for the new owners. I usually have one bag for each puppy to put everything in so all of their paperwork and other things are together and ready.

1. AKC papers should be completely filled out and ready for the new owners to sign.

2. Health documents from your vet should be ready for each pup.

3. Any brochures, pamphlets, etc. you received from your vet to give to new owners.

4. A cloth that has been rubbed on the mother and the littermates to help the pup through his first nights away from your home. Place this cloth (at least 1'x1') into a plastic baggy so it retains its scent.

5. At least one toy that the litter has played with.

6. Any medication that particular puppy needs.

7. A copy of Puppy Training 101, also by CA Wilkinson, the author of this book. New owners really appreciate this and it will give your puppies the best possible start in their new homes. Puppy Training 101 is available as an ebook at most major ebook merchandiser sites, or is available in print at https://www.createspace.com/4151742.

8. Small bag of the puppy food you feed the litter; at least enough to get the puppy through a couple of feedings. Also supply the owners with what brand you feed.

9. Your vet's name and phone number in case they have any questions or are in need of a good quality veterinarian.

10. A bottle of water from your home. Most people don't think water is a big deal but a difference in water from different cities can cause diarrhea in a puppy.

11. Have the health contract filled in as much as possible. Make sure they sign two copies, one for you and one for them.

12. Any special instructions for their particular puppy. This could include next worming, amount to feed, any medications to give or apply, etc.

This may seem like a lot to give and do, but doing so shows that you really care about your pups, where they're going, and that you plan on checking on them in the future. The things I send home with new owners fills the bag but my pups are worth it, even if they're not with me.

###

BIBLIOBRAPHY

Finder Harris, Beth J., 1993. Breeding a Litter: The Complete Book of Prenatal and Postnatal Care

Skidmore, Brenda & McConnell, Patricia B., 1996. Puppy Primer

The Monks of New Skete, 1991. The Art of Raising a Puppy

Other Books by CA Wilkinson

Puppy Training 101

The Little Book of Puppy Names

CPSIA information can be obtained at www.ICGtesting.com
Printed in the USA
LVOW12s2115261213

367018LV00014B/239/P

9 781483 905464